50 STATES TO CELEBRATE

Celebrating
NORTH CAROLINA

For information about permission to reproduce selections from this book,
write to Permissions, Houghton Mifflin Harcourt Publishing Company,
215 Park Avenue South, New York, New York 10003.

www.hmhco.com

The text of this book is set in Weidemann.
The display type is set in Bernard Gothic.
The illustrations are drawn with pencil and colored digitally.
The maps are pen, ink, and watercolor.

Photograph of gray squirrel on page 32 © 2013 by Photodisc/Getty Images
Photograph of northern cardinal on page 32 © 2013 by John J. Mosesso/life.nbii.gov
Photograph of flowering dogwood on page 32 © 2013 by April Robinson/Cutcaster

Library of Congress Cataloging-in-Publication Data
Bauer, Marion Dane.
Celebrating North Carolina / by Marion Dane Bauer ; illustrated by C. B. Canga.
p. cm. — (Green light readers level 3) (50 states to celebrate)
ISBN 978-0-544-28827-0 paperback
ISBN 978-0-544-28875-1 paper over board
1. North Carolina—Juvenile literature. I. Canga, C. B., illustrator. II. Title.
F254.3.B37 2014
975.6—dc23
2013050133

Manufactured in China
SCP 10 9 8 7 6 5 4 3 2 1
4500473726

50 STATES TO CELEBRATE

Celebrating
NORTH CAROLINA

Written by **Marion Dane Bauer**
Illustrated by **C. B. Canga**

Green Light Readers
Houghton Mifflin Harcourt
Boston   New York

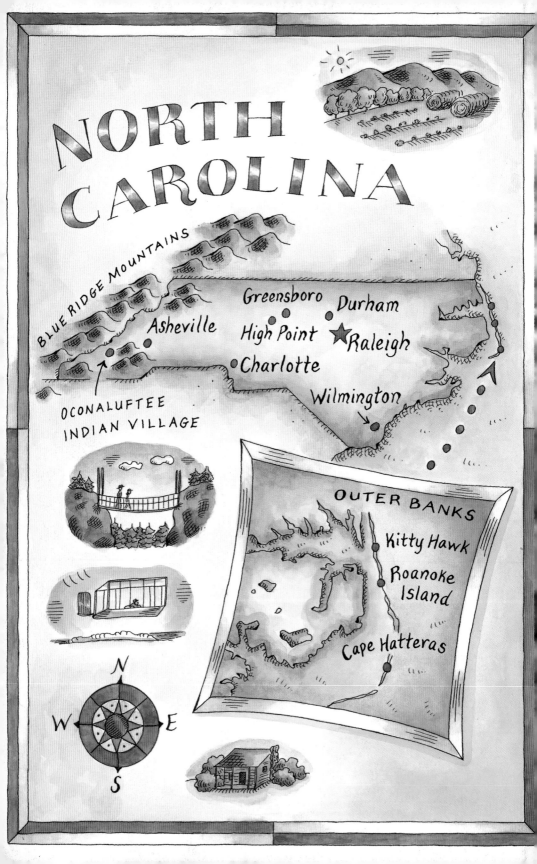

Hi! I'm Mr. Geo.

I'm visiting a state in the Southeast.

Just smell those flowering dogwood trees!

Do you know where I am?

If you guessed North Carolina, you're right!

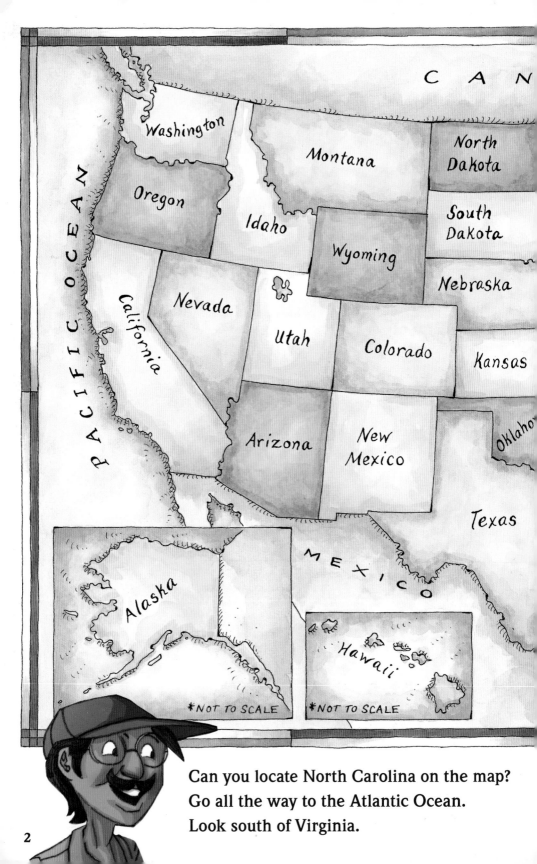

Can you locate North Carolina on the map?
Go all the way to the Atlantic Ocean.
Look south of Virginia.

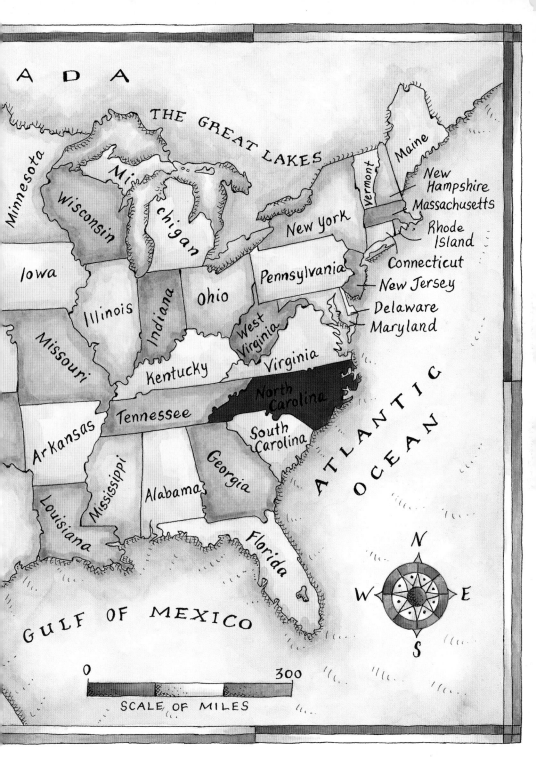

Now look east of Tennessee, then north
of South Carolina and Georgia.
That's North Carolina.

3

I'm starting my visit at Cape Hatteras on the
Outer Banks.
Here I am at the top of the tallest brick
lighthouse in the country.
I climbed 257 steps to get up here!
Whew!

The long sandy islands off the coast of North
Carolina are called the Outer Banks.

There are several more lighthouses
along the Outer Banks.
I don't think I'll climb them all, though!

The Outer Banks are a great place to play.
At Jockey's Ridge State Park we can go
sandboarding.
We can roll down sand **dunes** and fly kites.
Whish! Whoosh! Wow!

So many ships have sunk in Cape Hatteras
that it is sometimes called the Graveyard
of the Atlantic.

The Wright brothers flew the first airplane
from high dunes along the Outer Banks in 1903.
Later today I'm going to take a hang-gliding lesson.
Wish me a soft landing!

Wilbur and Orville Wright experimented
with gliders before they designed and flew
the first airplane near Kitty Hawk.

Arrrrr, mateys!
Come be a pirate with me.
We can dress up and sail along the
Carolina coast.

The clues on this map might
lead us to Blackbeard's treasure!

Blackbeard was a fierce pirate who attacked
ships and had hideouts on the North Carolina
coast in the early 1700s.

The Outer Banks are great for bird watching.
Hundreds of different kinds of birds live here.
Hundreds more **migrate** through in spring and fall.
Look! Isn't that a great crested flycatcher?

Wild horses called banker ponies live in
certain parts of the Outer Banks.

Many other animals live in coastal areas.
Yesterday, I saw a humpback whale.
Look! These baby loggerheads are getting ready
for their first swim!

Alligators can sometimes be found in
marshes, swamps, lakes, streams, and ponds
in North Carolina's coastal areas.

Native Americans were the first people in North Carolina.

The **Tuscarora** lived on the coastal plain.

The **Catawba** lived inland along a river, and the **Cherokee** lived in the mountains.

Did you know?

In 1838 thousands of Cherokee were forced to leave their homes in North Carolina. Their sad march to Oklahoma is called the **Trail of Tears**.

We can learn about old Cherokee crafts at
Oconaluftee Indian Village.
What I like best, though, is hearing ancient stories
by the campfire—and roasting marshmallows.
Whoops! I'm not going to eat that one!

The first English settlers arrived at
Roanoke Island in 1585.
Life was so hard that they sailed back to England.
Others came in 1587, but within three years
their colony was gone.

No one knows what happened to this Lost Colony. But at Roanoke Island Festival Park we can discover what it was like in those earlier times. I'm helping the **blacksmith** make kitchen tools.

North Carolina was one of the original 13 **colonies**.

On this rich land, colonial farms grew large.
New settlers depended on enslaved Africans
to work the fields and do many hard jobs.
Without freedom, the days were long and difficult.

Somerset Place lets us see what life
was like long ago on a southern **plantation**.
We can tour homes, barns, mills, and work areas.
We can make ropes, dip candles, and **gin cotton**.
We can reflect on the past.

The **Civil War** helped end slavery in
our country in 1865.

Today, North Carolina farms produce lots of sweet potatoes and tobacco. Peanuts and cotton, too.

Its hardwood forests are vast.
They provide lumber for the furniture industry,
as well as shade and beauty for miles and miles.

The city of High Point has long been a
center for furniture production.

If you like flowers, you'll love the
Azalea Festival in Wilmington.
The festival has more than flowers, though.
Parades, street fairs, music, and food!
Let's join the fun!

Or maybe you'd rather tour
Old Wilmington at night.
I could really use some company!

Other cities in North Carolina have lots to offer.
Asheville is home to many talented
artists and crafters.
This man is making me a banjo!

Raleigh, the state capital, is near many colleges, universities, and research centers. And when I'm in Charlotte, I love watching stock cars circle the track.
Zoom! Zoom! Zoom!

The NASCAR Hall of Fame is located in Charlotte.

Many folks in North Carolina love sports.
For professional basketball, they cheer for the
Charlotte Hornets.
Football fans have the Carolina Panthers, and
hockey fans love the Carolina Hurricanes.

But most everyone cheers loudest for their favorite college basketball teams!

Basketball superstar Michael Jordan got his start with the North Carolina Tar Heels at UNC–Chapel Hill.

25

What I admire most about North Carolina
is the varied landscape.
So many kinds of natural beauty!
I've traveled from beaches to coastal **plains**
to **plateaus** and now the mountains.

Today, I'm on the Mile High Swinging Bridge
at Grandfather Mountain.
It's the tallest peak in the
Blue Ridge Mountains of North Carolina.
Now, that's a spectacular sight!

North Carolina's coastal location sometimes
makes it a landing spot for **hurricanes** that
form in the Atlantic Ocean.

North Carolina's lush forests are home for many kinds of wildlife.

Black bears, white-tailed deer, and wild turkeys. And just look at that luna moth!

North Carolina has so much to enjoy.
I love its warm weather, lovely scenery,
busy cities, and deep history.
And so many places to visit!

But for my last night here,
I'm camping by this pretty waterfall.
And this time, I'm not going to burn
my marshmallow.
I promise!

Fast Facts
About North Carolina

Nickname: Tar Heel State; also, the Old North State.

State motto: To be, rather than to seem.

State capital: Raleigh.

Other major cities: Charlotte, Durham, Greensboro, Winston-Salem, Wilmington, Fayetteville, High Point.

Year of statehood: 1789.

State tree: Pine.

State mammal: Gray squirrel.   **State bird:** Northern cardinal.

State flower: Flowering dogwood.   **State flag:**

Population: According to the 2010 census, nearly 10 million people.

Fun fact: In 1587, Virginia Dare was the first English child to be born in America. It happened in the area that would later become North Carolina.

Dates in North Carolina History

1400s: Cherokee, Tuscarora, Catawba, Hatteras, Chowanoc, and other Native American people living in the area that is now North Carolina.

1585: First English colony established on Roanoke Island, followed by a second group of colonists in 1587.

1590: John White returns from getting supplies in England to find no colonists on Roanoke Island.

1650s: North Carolina's first permanent European settlement is established near Albemarle Sound.

1776: North Carolina declares independence from England with the other 12 American colonies.

1838: The U.S. government forces the Cherokee to leave their homeland in North Carolina and march west to what is now Oklahoma.

1861: North Carolina secedes from the Union at the start of the Civil War.

1868: North Carolina readmitted to Union.

1903: Wilbur and Orville Wright make the first successful powered airplane flight near Kitty Hawk.

1959: Research Triangle Park opens in an area between Raleigh, Durham, and Chapel Hill; it triggers an era of high-tech growth.

1960: Four African American college students protest segregation by sitting in at a lunch counter "for whites only" in Greensboro.

1999: Hurricanes Dennis and Floyd cause record flooding and environmental damage.

2006: The Carolina Hurricanes hockey team wins the Stanley Cup championship.

Activities

1. **LOCATE** the four states that border North Carolina. Then, **SAY** each state's name out loud.

2. **DESIGN** a sign that welcomes people to North Carolina. The sign will be on the highway, so it can be big. Include words and pictures that describe and show something special about the state.

3. **SHARE** two facts you learned about North Carolina with a family member or friend.

4. **PRETEND** you live in North Carolina and you have relatives from another state visiting for the first time. Your cousins have lots of questions about North Carolina. See if you can correctly answer the questions they have.

   a. **WHERE** is the country's tallest brick lighthouse located?

   b. **WHO** flew the first powered airplanes from high dunes in the Outer Banks?

   c. **WHEN** did the first English settlers arrive in North Carolina?

   d. **WHAT** are three farm products grown in North Carolina?

5. **UNJUMBLE** these words that have something to do with North Carolina. Write your answers on a separate sheet of paper.

   a. **KOOREAN** (HINT: an island)

   b. **DLBRKABECA** (HINT: a fierce pirate)

   c. **EEKOHECR** (HINT: a native American people)

   d. **LAZAAE** (HINT: a flower)

   e. **RNITRUUEF** (HINT: a product made in North Carolina)

Glossary

blacksmith: a person who makes tools and other objects out of iron by heating the iron and pounding it with a hammer. (p. 15)

Catawba: a Native American people who lived mainly in the middle of the state along the Catawba River. (p. 12)

Cherokee: Native American people who lived in the mountainous area of North Carolina. (p. 12)

Civil War: the war between the northern states and the southern states that helped end slavery in the United States. (p. 17)

colony: a settlement ruled by a different country (p. 15)

dune: a hill or ridge of sand that the wind has piled up. (p. 6)

gin cotton: to separate the seeds from the fibers of cotton by using a special machine called a gin. (p. 17)

hurricane: a powerful storm with heavy rains and winds of more than 74 miles per hour. (p. 27)

migrate: to move from one place to another. (p. 10)

Outer Banks: a series of long, narrow islands along the coast of North Carolina. (p. 4)

plain: a large flat area with few trees; a coastal plain is near the ocean. (p. 26)

plantation: a large farm where crops are grown. (p. 17)

plateau: a high area of land that can be flat or hilly on top. (p. 26)

sandboarding: riding across or down a sand dune on a board; a board sport that is popular in desert and coastal areas with sand dunes. (p. 6)

Trail of Tears: The forced movement of the Cherokee people from their lands in North Carolina to Oklahoma in 1838 and 1839 by the United States government. (p. 12)

Tuscarora: a Native American people who lived mainly in the coastal plain region of North Carolina. (p. 12)

Answers to activities on page 34:

Answers to Activities on page 34: 1) Virginia, South Carolina, Georgia, and Tennessee; 2) Sign drawings will vary; 3) Answers will vary; 4a) Cape Hatteras in the Outer Banks, 4b) Wilbur and Orville Wright—the Wright Brothers, 4c) 1585, 4d) sweet potatoes, cotton, peanuts, and/or tobacco; 5a) ROANOKE, 5b) BLACKBEARD, 5c) CHEROKEE, 5d) AZALEA, 5e) FURNITURE.